Another Cup of My Coffee

Lessons for Life and Leadership

Scott H. Dearduff

ISBN: 9781499799729
ISBN-13: 9781499799729

DEDICATION

This book is dedicated to the mentors and coaches that influenced my life and leadership development. There are many who positively added to my development and taught me valuable lessons that I tried to bring to leadership situations throughout my life.

CONTENTS

ACKNOWLEDGMENTS

Special thanks to the people who reviewed and edited this book for publication; Kenneth Woodcock, Rob Dearduff, Jeff Wepner, Robert Simpson, Lynn Brennard, Reid Horton, Deepthi Pillai, Mark Lankford, and Kirk Pontow. The time and effort they willingly put into this project was invaluable. And as usual, I would like to thank my family, especially my wife, for putting up with my dedication to bringing this project to publication.

Dearduff

FORWARD

This book was written with the intent of sharing leadership lessons gained from a life lived to the fullest. The author believes that hard work, determination, dedication, and living by core values of integrity, honesty, loyalty, and belief in oneself, can lead to success in life and work. We hope the factual stories in this book provide the reader with some level of learning, and provides ideas on how to use these lessons in your own life. Happy reading!

1
Slow Down and Ask the Next Question

Leaders want to have all the answers, be responsive and handle things for their followers. Unfortunately, you may not have the right answer following the initial question or may take inappropriate actions based on the limits of what you know. The best plan in many situations may be to slow down and dig deeper before providing incorrect information or taking action that is not correct.

People want leaders to resolve their issues just as much as leaders desire to fix things for them. But, unless there are bullets flying, something is on fire, or someone is bleeding (life-threatening situations) there is no need to provide immediate responses in all situations. If bullets, blood, or fire are present, you definitely need to act or answer promptly. Failing to do so will have dire consequences. Short of a life-threatening situation, there will be time for additional clarification.

While deployed on a combat mission in Iraq, an Air Force unit was alerted to complete a complex and dangerous mission into Iran for humanitarian relief. The mission required an aircrew and security team to enter the country, delivery critical cargo, and depart without and problems. The team's presence would not be acknowledged once they entered into Iran since there were no diplomatic relations between the U.S. and Iran. If something happened while inside Iran, a rescue attempt by a special operations team located at an undisclosed classified location was the only hope.

Mission details were shared verbally by the intelligence specialists. There was equipment to prepare, notifications to make, and a concept of operations to develop for actions after landing. Time was limited, causing assumptions to be made in preparation for the scheduled departure. The window of opportunity to complete the mission was small, and there would only be one chance.

Hours later the C-130 tactical military transport plane crossed the border of Iran at 20,000 feet, fully loaded with 60,000 pounds of cargo. Entering enemy airspace drew attention from Iranian fighter aircraft that aligned on both wings. The C-130 pilot called the team leader to the cockpit with night vision goggles and instructed him to identify the enemy aircraft who failed to acknowledge radio calls for identification. The leader quickly determined that a Mig-29 was flying close to the left wing and another was flying similarly on the right wing. There was no way to tell the aircraft's intent due to the lack of communications.

Weapons were visible on each wing of the Mig-29s. The pilot and crew were sweating from the stress of the potentially volatile situation. The tension was thick and everyone prepared for the worst once they landed.

The scene at the airfield was chaotic and stressful. There was limited lighting that restricted the security team's ability to detect people who moved around the aircraft uncontrollably. The aircraft came to a stop and the cargo bay doors opened exposing the true chaos of the situation. Within seconds of the C-130 coming to a stop, unidentified people surrounded the aircraft, demanding to be given the cargo. People began removing items from the cargo bay and demanded to get on board. Language barriers prevented proper communications and added to the threat that one of the locals could attempt to stow away on the aircraft and leave the country with the U.S. Forces. The security team leader decided that a show of force with weapons was the only option to gain some semblance of order and move the locals away from the back of the aircraft.

A representative of the U.S. Embassy in Kuwait arrived and directed the distribution of cargo from the plane. He also directed the security team leader to put away all the weapons that were outside of the aircraft. The team leader initially debated his direction, then received a more passionate direction to move all weapons back inside of the plane which he complied with. The security team maintained concealed weapons for personal safety. The Embassy representative informed the crew that the cargo would be stolen before it left the airfield and the only thing that mattered was to empty the cargo and prepare for takeoff.

The cargo was unloaded and the crew retreated inside the aircraft for departure. Soon the pilot informed the security team leader they were being detained because the airfield authority was demanding more money for a landing fee. The tension among all crew members rose with the possibility that Iranian forces were detaining them. Thoughts of escape and survival ran through everyone's minds as they developed a solution. After some tense debate, the pilot promised the local authorities that he would arrange more money for the landing fee if the aircraft was allowed to depart. Moments later the pilot started engines and the entire team was told to strap in for a quick departure.

Exiting Iran came with another Mig-29 fighter escort until the C-130 reached the border of Iranian airspace. Once safely out of the country, the crew felt relief and a sense of accomplishment. Everyone prepared to celebrate completing the dangerous mission once they landed because it seemed like everything went exactly as planned.

Landing on the friendly airfield in southern Iraq controlled by U.S. Forces, the C-130 taxied to a parking spot where a small group of military leaders awaited. The security team and aircrew all expected to be welcomed back with some level of celebration and seeing the crowd seemed to confirm those thoughts. Unfortunately the celebration was replaced by frustration and immediate questions about what took place while in Iran.

The security team leader was informed they were all under suspicion of causing an international incident and the general was demanding answers. Everyone was quickly moved to the headquarters where the general and several staff members waited. Entering the large conference room, it was obvious that everyone was on edge and the meeting was not a celebration of any kind.

As the discussion began, the general's comments indicated that he was never made aware of the mission or that any of his Airmen were tasked to fly into Iran. He noted that he received a call from the combined air operations center asking him to provide details of an international incident caused by one of his crews in Iran. He shared that when he told the command that he did not have crews in Iran and they must be mistaken, he was informed that he was actually wrong. When he learned that a team of his Airmen and one of his combat aircraft were tasked with this critical mission and nobody informed him, he was justifiably upset. He demanded answers from everyone in the room.

An intelligence specialist spoke up and informed the general that during the pre-mission briefing they overlooked a note about keeping all firearms inside the aircraft. He went on to share that the security team was not provided with that specific rule of engagement, and made the decision to use their firearms for the safety of the entire crew, leading to the claim of an international incident. The general grew more frustrated with every sentence.

The colonel in charge of the operations group told the general that he took responsibility for not informing the general about the mission. The general shared his displeasure with hearing that accountability statement. When he was done telling the colonel how disappointed he was that a mistake of that nature could be made, the general went around the room asking each person why they failed him. There were no good answers and nobody seemed willing to attempt to find one. The general concluded the meeting by relieving everyone of duty and initiating an investigation.

It took a week for the investigation to finish and clear the crew from responsibility for the international incident, allowing them to return to full duty. Although everyone returned to normal combat operations, there were some valuable lessons learned from the event. Above all else, it was clear that everything moved fast in the planning process. Each person involved was so focused on what they were about to do that they failed to ask questions for clarity. The briefers hurried through the mission orders causing them to miss critical details. The crew was focused on flying into a hostile country and dealt with the possibilities of being shot down. And the security team was concerned about the safety and survival aspects of the dangerous mission. But the hurried nature of the preparations led to the omission of vital information. At any point during the process anyone could have taken a moment to slow down and ask the next question.

That simple action could have prevented the negative attention of the international incident. And anyone from the planning team to the colonels involved in the process could have taken time to slow down and realize that it would be smart to notify the general about this dangerous mission. By not slowing down and asking those questions, mistakes were made that negatively impacted everyone involved.

Another Cup of My Coffee

Lesson 1

Slow Down and Ask the Next Question

Take the time to gather appropriate information before making decisions and taking dangerous or serious actions

Key points for leaders:

Slow down to gain understanding

- Determine immediacy of the question/answer
- Be inquisitive before blurting out an answer
- Clarify points the other person is making
- Ask if they know how to solve the problem
- Understand contingency plans may be necessary
- Consider information from diverse perspectives

Don't assume you know everything

- Don't fall victim to the culture of assumptions
- Determine what you already know or can learn
- Engage and trust subject matter experts
- Stay focused on the primary objective
- Don't hurry (unless life or death matters)
- Ask team members if they have suggestions

Understand the impact of social media usage

- Once you hit send, you cannot take it back
- Don't post anything you would not say in person
- Generational differences create distance with leaders

Final Thoughts

In some situations, the person asking the question is simply trying to gain information or may be asking in hopes that you will make a decision for them. If the decision belongs to them, focus on what they are asking and continue asking questions until they come up with a solution. If they cannot provide insight or are frustrated from not being able to figure it out, rather than provide the answer to them, guide them to the solution.

By taking the time to slow down and ask the next question, you may avoid embarrassing situations later on. If you fail to slow down, you may act or provide an answer based on the limited information you have, which could be the wrong answer. If that happens, you will spend a lot of time fixing your mistakes like the team members in the story.

What is the next question?

- The situation will dictate your next questions
- Once the question is answered, ask another
- Keep asking questions until you find the answer
- Continue to reveal all relevant information
- Examples;
    o What else do we know?
    o How did this happen?
    o What resources are needed?
    o When does this need to be completed?
    o What are the obstacles to completion?

2
Relevance Begins with Presence

Every leader will get opportunities to act in the performance of their duties. How you act and how effective your actions are will determine the level of success you will achieve. If you make little to no effort to lead people, chances are you will be ineffective or potentially fail in your leadership responsibilities. To increase your chance of success as a leader in the world of modern technology, a great starting point is being present with your people whenever possible.

Working with a team in a foreign country is difficult because of the language barriers, cultural differences, and professional values displayed while performing duties. Clear lines of communication are essential to ensure understanding by everyone involved; not an easy task when dealing with friendly foreign nations.

During a six-month planning process to organize a critical joint response between U.S. Forces and the host nation security force, all hands were on deck to ensure success. However, the director of U.S. security forces skipped meetings to focus on other priorities. He scanned meeting minutes and passed on opportunities to ask questions or give directions. The exercise required 45 members of the two security forces to come together during a simulated attack on nuclear resources and defeat a determined enemy. The response was graded on a time frame considered a pass or fail situation. If the forces failed to meet the time specifications, the entire situation would be repeated until it was completed successfully. If the overall exercise was a failure, those who were responsible for the security forces would likely lose their positions and receive disciplinary or corrective action. The stakes were high.

After the months of planning and preparing, everyone who was directly involved felt they were ready to execute the exercise and meet the expectations. The only person who was not on board and ready to execute was the director of the U.S. security forces. He remained absent throughout the preparations.

When the day arrived, the director suddenly decided to become engaged and started asking questions. At the beginning of the day he noticed things he was not happy with, and injected his thoughts into the conversation; attempting to force last minute changes into the exercise. The exercise coordinator, one of his direct reports, was confused at first why the director wanted to change things so late in the process after not getting involved during all of the preparation work. He reminded the director that a great deal of planning and coordination went into the exercise and his lack of earlier engagement indicated agreement with all planned actions. He added that careful consideration was taken to ensure all leaders and foreign dignitaries could view the exercise and gain confidence in how the joint team worked toward mission accomplishment. Many hours were spent developing exercise objectives to ensure a successful event without the director's input.

Critical to the overall success of the exercise was to make sure the foreign dignitaries were in the right place and at the right time to view the important parts of the exercise. Changing details just before the exercise started would cause confusion, negatively impact the outcome of the exercise, and change how it was received by the viewing parties. The entire exercise could fail because of last minute adjustments. When the director was informed that it was too late to make his changes, he vehemently disagreed. His emotions took over and he became angry. At one point he became argumentative in front of some of the viewing party, causing tension all around.

An uncomfortable conversation took place with the two leaders standing nose to nose. The director relayed that he was not happy and demanded changes be made. Counter-arguments were made about prior coordination and timing of changes, and that unless there were safety concerns, changes would not be made. The director made a last-ditch effort to sway the exercise and have his changes implemented. He stated, "I wasn't asking you to make the changes, I am telling you." For the good of the exercise, with intent to conduct a positive engagement with the foreign nation, the exercise coordinator stood his ground and refused to make the changes. That decision was made at the risk of losing his job.

The director made a final effort to change the plan, he said, "Just do what I told you to do, and do it now." The exercise coordinator refused, and told him, "You had the opportunity to provide your inputs and changes over the past few months. But, because you were not present during meetings and took no interest in the development of the objectives, it's too late to include your ideas now. Your ideas are not relevant at this point."

The director responded that he should fire the coordinator on the spot and take over the exercise himself. But the reality and gravity of the situation became clear, and he realized that his lack of presence put him at a disadvantage. He could not take over the exercise and make it successful because he was absent during the planning meetings and had no details about the exercise. Rather than embarrass himself at that point, the director departed without another word. The exercise proceeded as planned and the results were tremendous. Everyone involved felt the objectives were met or exceeded, and the foreign dignitaries who observed the exercise were pleased.

Hours after the exercise was complete and everyone returned to normal operations, the director decided that he should apologize for being in the wrong by trying to make last minute changes. During follow-on discussions the director acknowledged that his lack of presence contributed to the problem. He also admitted that he knew this was a critical exercise and he should have given his time and attention during the planning phase.

His thinking was flawed and led to frustration for himself and the others involved. He allowed himself to believe that he could walk in and change anything he wanted at the last minute without complications. He lacked understanding that relevance begins with presence and it almost ruined a major event.

Another Cup of My Coffee

Lesson 2

Relevance Begins with Presence

Leaders must be seen and heard to have positive impact

<u>Key points for leaders:</u>

Be present physically and mentally

- Insist on presence at all leadership levels
- Set an example for attendance and conduct
- Meet people regularly where people work
- Be engaged in processes from start to finish
- Meet virtually when not geographically present

Lack of presence leads to lack of success

- Leaders lose the attention of their people
- Leaders become isolated from their people
- People become less responsive to the leader
- People feel detached from the organization
- Communications are difficult to maintain

Eliminate distractions by putting your phone away

- Impacts influence on people at work and home
- Shows respect or lack of respect for other people
- Being distracted show a genuine lack of interest

Final Thoughts

Some obstacles work against leaders being present with all of their people. In the fast-paced world today, leaders have to use technology to overcome a lack of physical presence with their people and teams. When you cannot be there, you can still be present through virtual meetings, tele-presence, or at a minimum, communicate with team members by phone, through email or other electronic means. Don't let geographic distance stop you from being present. Just don't ever rely on email as a leadership tool.

Geographic distance can complicate matters:

- Communicate regularly using technology
- Host a conference at your physical location
- Spend quality time with people during visits
- Follow up on questions and offer sound advice

Shift operations create distance:

- Break your routine and work when they work
- Adjust meetings to their working schedules
- Put people before paperwork every time
- Praise/recognize people when you are with them
- Delegate meetings and commitments to other leaders
- Flexible scheduling helps maintain work-life balance

3
You Have Been So Advised

Every leader should strive to be an expert in their chosen career or business and be highly engaged in all aspects of their responsibility. There will be times when your expertise will be challenged by others and your advice will be devalued or discarded. When that happens, you may find yourself with few options and the instinct to give in or give up may be strong. But don't give up and walk away without offering your best advice to help the situation.

A manager was hired to lead a team of armed security officers in the private sector and inherited several problems that plagued the team for several years. One of the most critical needs was to locate and operate a training room that would enhance the response capability of the security officers. A proper training room would go a long way to improve professional training for critical incident response.

The team consisted of well-trained military and law enforcement veterans. They were motivated to do a good job but were more dissimilar than they were alike. Each of the team members was trained at different platforms with diverse missions. Those differences exposed holes in the consistency of the organization's training program. A primary objective for the training officer and manager was to mold the team into a cohesive unit with a standardized set of skills.

The training program lacked creativity and failed to challenge the officers. Conducting realistic training was restricted because it took place in a small classroom co-located with several business classrooms where students prepared for insurance exams. Security training required the escalation of force which comes with raised voices. The sounds from security training were disruptive to the insurance classes and several campus leaders became concerned. The rise in a threat of workplace violence required an increase in the intensity of the training, but that could not take place where it was located. Something needed to change fast to keep up with the emerging threat. The future of the training program depended on finding a better location to train the officers on verbal de-escalation, defensive tactics, and active shooter response.

The training program also required the use of a firearms simulator that challenged the officers in response to a stimulus presented during on-screen scenarios. To effectively engage each scenario, the officer needed room to maneuver and unlimited restrictions on giving verbal commands. The current training room did not provide those aspects, negatively impacting the overall training for the officers. These shortfalls in the training program drove the manager to search for a new training location to enhance the program and meet mission objectives.

An initial review of the massive building complex revealed no space available. But a building expansion project was underway that would open some new options for space. Searching through the new space revealed a room that was far removed from the business area, was soundproof, and provided ample room for all of the training gear and equipment. The manager requested a meeting with the executive director for facilities to see if he could gain ownership of the space for a training room.

During the initial meeting the executive director was clear that he was not open to the creation of a training room and he stood firm that the space was earmarked for storage of materials and equipment. He said that all areas of the expansion project were spoken for and there was no place for a training room. He was clear that there was no room on the space utilization priority list. He was not known for giving in and seemed determined to maintain his position in this case.

The manager shared his concern that without a proper training space they could be setting the company up for liability if a critical incident happened and the officers responded poorly. The executive director paid attention but was still not convinced. The manager reminded him that following an officer involved shooting, there would be a comprehensive review of the response, the equipment, and the training of the responding officer. The actions of the incident could also be challenged in a courtroom if someone claimed wrongful death of injury because of poor response by the officers. He went on to say that as the manager he would be called to testify and that training would be a topic of discussion. He stated that under oath he would be required to share that the responding officer was not properly trained because the training room had limitations that prevented proper training. The executive director knew that he was being given advice on the possible ramifications if the officers were not properly trained.

The manager provided advice to the executive director in hopes that it would lead to a smart business decision. He never told the executive director that his advice was given to prevent problems on the company's worst day, but it was very clear. He also never said that he would be documenting the advice that was given and not heeded, but that also seemed apparent.

The manager concluded that it would be easy for a lawyer to determine that a lack of training contributed to the poor response and possible wrongful death. It was clear the company would be at great risk and likely be held accountable financially. The room was silent. The executive director knew at that moment that he was being provided information and advice, which if ignored, would make him liable in a wrongful death situation. He said, "Let me see what I can do." The next day the executive director called the manager to his office to show him the new training space on the building plans.

Although the words, "You have been so advised," were never said during the conversation, the executive director was an astute leader who knew the security manager was advising him toward a smart decision. The reality of a situation ending badly was something the executive director did not want to be saddled with because he placed storing furniture over training armed officers for active shooter response. He weighed the outcomes and knew that he needed to take the advice and ensure the company committed to training the officers.

The executive director's decision to dedicate training space established a state-of-the-art training room. The security training program blossomed with the expanded capabilities and the executive director received personal recognition every time the room was shown to others. His choice to take sound advice from the manager paid dividends for years.

Lesson 3

You Have Been So Advised

Advise your leaders with positive intent to impact their decisions

Key points for leaders:

Facts get you everywhere, emotions get you nowhere

- Leave emotions out of your advice and discussions
- Let the facts of the situation speak for themselves
- Avoid assumptions and speculation
- Avoid personal bias while giving advice
- Do your homework, discuss all the options
- Be honest and direct, don't be a "yes man"

Document your advice, even if not used

- Record information from the discussion
- Annotate reasoning for your advice and the decision
- Document facts for future review by others
- Be prepared to re-address the situation later on

Be prepared that your advice may not be used

- Provide strong discussion points for consideration
- Not all advice will fit the leader's solution set
- Support decisions publically even if you don't agree

Final Thoughts

Sometimes you will give sound advice and make recommendations based on the facts of what your experience tells you is appropriate. That advice may not be what the other person wants to hear. When that happens, don't take it personal, just continue to support them.

The advice you give must be based on facts and not your emotions. Share your professional opinion and don't be offended if it's not accepted. If the person receiving your advice fails to heed it, and the situation goes bad later, they own the consequences of their decision. If they deflect and blame you, their argument cannot stand against your unheeded and well documented advice.

How you deliver the message of "***You have been so advised***" can be taken wrong and the receiver may get defensive. Remember that one comment taken the wrong way can ruin a professional relationship. Use it sparingly. If you say it at all, insert the comment into the discussion before ending. That will put the receiver on notice that you gave the advice you thought was best for the situation. And although you do not agree with their decision, you will support them publicly.

4
Courage is a Great Motivator

Handling leadership responsibility requires qualities that are not guaranteed and take time and effort to develop. As leadership traits grow within a person, they earn respect and loyalty from their followers. Courageous actions and decisions are at the top of that list of critical leadership qualities. People understand that leading and decision-making are not always easy but they seek leaders who can make tough decisions. Courageous decisions are required during normal circumstances just as much as they are in difficult times. As a leader, being ready and willing to display courage at all times will serve you well.

Leading in combat required leaders to stand up to enemy action, maintain discipline under extreme conditions, and remain strong in front of the troops. Not every situation required battlefield courage and not every leader understood the need to show courage. One leader held responsibility for 50 armed combatants whose duty required them to face the enemy head-on each day while defending the base. She briefed her team on incidents or attacks from the previous shift, inspected them to ensure a high state of readiness, and provided them with current intelligence reports for the day ahead. Standing in front of that adrenaline-filled team of warriors was tough for any leader, but some considered it even tougher for a female security force supervisor. Kelly was up to the task, willingly accepted the challenges of her position, and performed admirably day in and day out. As her team responded to enemy attacks on the base, she was out front making tough decisions while protecting thousands of Americans who served on the base.

One afternoon her boss, a security force manager, made contact with the command chief, the unit's senior leader, and asked if he could come to the office with Kelly and relay a major problem that suddenly arose. Every day in combat brought new challenges, problems, and unusual circumstances that leaders had to deal with. The chief was ready for whatever this major problem was and he anxiously awaited their arrival. Because of the high level of responsibility the chief handled each day, people only brought the toughest situations to him for resolution. He figured this must be a difficult problem that needed his attention.

When they arrived at the office, the manager walked in and told the chief that he should prepare himself. Wondering what this could be about, he told the manager to bring Kelly in. As she entered the office it was obvious that something was different. Her physical appearance caught the chief's attention and it was painfully obvious that Kelly was significantly impacted by her appearance. There was a short period of silence without Kelly or her manager saying a word. Remaining calm and showing no reaction, the chief said, "I don't understand what the problem is." Stunned by the statement, Kelly told the chief that she was not going to be able to complete her duties because she was no longer able to get the necessary make-up she needed to cover her vitiligo, a skin disorder that causes white patches of skin to appear on the face and other body parts. She went on to share that standing in front of her team and providing leadership would be too difficult. The chief stated again, "I don't understand the problem."

Both Kelly and her manager looked at each other wondering if the chief could see her newly revealed appearance. It was obvious that Kelly was struggling with how she could complete her duties and not be embarrassed in front of her team. Although the chief realized that Kelly was covering her skin before that day, and that she never faltered in her duties, he chose not to take sympathy on her. He did not believe that her appearance would have any impact on her performance and ability to lead. In the chief's eyes, she did not need to hide behind a mask to be courageous and handle her duties.

Still stunned, Kelly asked the chief if he could see her face. He told her, "I'm not sure what the problem is. I see Kelly standing in front of me, a strong leader who is committed to taking care of her team and completing a difficult mission." She was speechless, standing silently wondering what to say next. Kelly asked the chief what she should do since she would be unable to get more make-up for several weeks. He told her that she was to go back to her team, lead them courageously and be who she was. He reminded Kelly that he didn't see anything different than he saw the previous day and that everyone else would respond the same. The chief came out from behind his desk, gave her a battle hug, and sent her back to work.

Standing in front of her team just minutes later, Kelly never faltered and never failed. She led with courage, never once asking for mercy and never making excuses. As the weeks passed and she finally received the make-up required to cover her skin, she decided that it was no longer necessary. People accepted her for who she was and respected her for the courage it took to lead in combat while dealing with a personal situation that negatively impacted her confidence and self-esteem. For the remainder of the year she never again hid behind the mask, performing and thriving as the amazing person that she was. She led her teams while charging headlong into enemy action. Many team members took courage from her example, going on to earn combat medals for courageous service. Overall, her courageous leadership provided motivation for her team, led to the protection of military aircraft and saved hundreds of lives.

The daily display of courage exhibited by Kelly transcended to other leaders. People watched her stand tall in front of her followers during difficult situations. Many took strength from her actions and the ability she displayed while remaining in control. The chief regularly met with Kelly to ensure she knew he trusted her and stood behind her actions. At the completion of her combat tour, many struggled to watch her leave.

The chief served in other combat leadership positions over the next four years and on two occasions encountered Kelly while she served in other leadership positions. Each time they met, the chief took pride in seeing that Kelly had not changed, had not returned to the leader behind the mask. Kelly always stood tall as a dedicated leader and motivator. Her courage provided reassurance that personal appearance is insignificant in determining a person's ability to perform and lead. The troops who worked for her demonstrated high levels of loyalty to this courageous leader.

Lesson 4

Courage is a Great Motivator

Do not worry about other people judging you

Key points for leaders:

Stand firm in the face of difficult situations

- Take action regardless of perceived shortcomings
- Let your abilities drive your actions
- Don't let opinions of others limit your actions
- Remain confident in your leadership ability
- Use mentors for advice when facing challenges
- Reflect on and address areas in your personal life

Don't shrink from responsibility

- Difficult situations bring out the best in leaders
- Overcome personal issues to remain in charge
- Show others you can handle any situation
- Be vulnerable when needed, strong always
- Be willing to take on the toughest jobs
- Don't allow social media judgement to impact you

Final Thoughts

Every leader has the ability to act based on their internal courage. It's OK to be unsure about how you or your actions will be received, but you cannot let that control how you perform. When you are faced with something difficult, but remain strong in your conviction, followers will develop a deep respect for your leadership ability.

Others grow their courage based on your actions

- Followers will succeed by emulating you
- Confidence results in motivation for others
- Followers will respect you for displaying courage
- Team productivity will be positively impacted

It would have been easy for Kelly to step away from her leadership responsibility, use her personal situation as an excuse to quit and let someone else take her place. Instead she took courage from the chief's response to her perceived issue. When he told her that he only saw the strong leader standing in front of him, she grew confident that she would be able to lead as she was. Kelly's display of courage and resilience set an amazing example for many others to emulate.

5

Other People Determine Your Legacy

All leaders leave a legacy after they are gone. People will think of you based on the things they saw you do, what they heard you say, and how you took care of them. All of these things make up your legacy. Leaders who understand that serving others is important to success and who take time to get to know their people will find higher levels of success. If people liked the way you handled your leadership responsibility, you will leave a lasting legacy filled with positive thoughts that will be carried on by others. If your leadership style was based on negative actions or self-serving actions, the legacy you leave will reflect that negativism. Leaders who are clearly more interested in their own success will leave a bad legacy in the minds of the people they were privileged to lead.

A security director with two hundred people under his supervision spent countless hours getting to know the people he led even though his duties required maximum effort. The investment of time in getting to know people would present many opportunities to develop a positive legacy. His actions also told people that he placed as much emphasis on taking care of them as he did with completing the mission. People learned quickly that he believed taking care of the people would relate to taking care of the mission. Caring about them helped when problems arose because they knew they had someone to rely on who would genuinely care about their issues.

One November day just before Thanksgiving one of his long-time followers walked into the office with a stressed look on his face. Without saying a single word, Tom sat down. Gathering himself, he said, "They just diagnosed me with stage four Hodgkin's Lymphoma." There was silence in the room as the director digested what Tom just shared. Knowing it was some kind of cancer, the director said he was unsure what that meant. Tom responded that it was a form of cancer that was attacking his body aggressively.

In the minutes that followed, Tom described his diagnosis of cancer in his lymph nodes, chest, and stomach. His doctor told him he had six months to live at best, and that he should immediately retire from the military, sell all of his personal items, and travel the world or do things he always wanted to do before he died. The director was not prepared for this conversation and was unsure how to deal with cancer or the finality of the diagnosis. The only response he could muster was, "I'm not standing for that diagnosis, let's get a second opinion."

Tom agreed and the director asked for help preventing his immediate retirement to allow him a chance to fight the cancer. They walked into the boss' office where they described what was going on. The director asked for some leniency and requested time to ensure they could get a second opinion. After a short conversation and more details, they were granted time to figure out a plan that would allow Tom to get treatment and return to work if he was physically able. In the weeks that followed, a second doctor agreed to let Tom undergo experimental treatment to fight this aggressive cancer. Tom held off selling his house and other goods at the encouragement of the director in order to maintain a sense of stability in his life.

The initial six months of the treatment plan required Tom to move across the state where he could get the medical care he needed. After two weeks of treatment and working in a made-up position with a local organization, Tom contacted the director and asked if he could return to work and travel back and forth for treatment to improve his morale. He shared that being a part of a team that he had no connection with was causing him daily bouts of depression and it was actually impeding his recovery. He said that his doctor would approve the plan as long as his bloodwork showed positive results.

Pitching this plan to the boss was not easy. It would require Tom to work Monday, fly across the state on Tuesday, attend intense treatment on Wednesday, fly back home on Thursday, work that afternoon, and all day Friday. The organization was tasked with national level responsibility for critical resources and had never before accepted such a radical plan for any of its team members. The director developed a work plan that would support Tom's schedule and contribute important work toward mission accomplishment. When the director notified Tom that his plan was approved and he could begin the following week, there was immediate relief. He began making arrangement to fly home following the next treatment.

While the next six months were difficult on Tom, the treatments went well and the doctors reported a miraculous turn-around in his cancer diagnosis. The director visited him several times at personal expense while he was undergoing treatment to make sure he was getting what he needed. At the six-month check-up, Tom was cleared for full duty and identified as cancer-free. Many in the organization were surprised to see Tom return to full duty after his initial diagnosis. When he was asked how that happened, he would often say, "My director cared about me and remained open to the idea that I could beat cancer, gave me purpose and here I am." That statement told people that he credited the director with caring for him to the point that he could maintain a normal life.

The reward for caring about Tom and providing him with a life-purpose, was 10 more years of service in the organization filled with promotions and awards. Tom exceeded his own expectations for his career and proved to everyone that he could overcome a huge life obstacle.

He also lived 17 productive years before the cancer finally returned and took his life. As the cancer returned and his health rapidly declined, it was clear that Tom was at peace with the path his life took. Tom's final words to the director were filled with appreciation for the care and concern provided in allowing him to extend his life. Tom thanked him for caring and believing in him. Tom's final words to the director indicated that a positive legacy was formed by everyone he knew just because of how his situation was handled.

The director's willingness to care for Tom, despite high organizational performance goals, showed that he cared about people as much, if not more, than the mission. He could have brushed Tom aside to focus on mission objectives and advancing his own career. Instead, he took time each day to care for one of his followers during the most difficult time of his life.

Other followers watched the director care for Tom during this difficult journey, solidifying his legacy as a caring leader whose total commitment to the mission was only matched by his total commitment to the people within the organization.

Lesson 5

Other People Determine Your Legacy

Opinions are formed based on how they see you perform

Key points for leaders:

Caring leaders show genuine interest in people/family

- Take care of people, people take care of the mission
- Put maximum effort into their individual needs
- Help them meet individual goals and objectives
- Support their ideas and challenge their ability
- Drive them to pursue growth and development
- People are the most valuable resource

Positively impact the most people possible

- Establish a culture focused on taking care of people
- People remember how you make them feel
- Everyone can learn something from you
- Be careful not to focus on a few favorite people
- Make everyone feel valued and important
- Selflessness should be your everyday standard

Final Thoughts

You have little ability to determine how you are remembered by those who follow in your footsteps. Your actions during the time that you serve as a leader will be viewed and judged by your followers, leading them to determine your legacy.

If you positively impact people along the years, there will be a trail of success filled with your followers. The amount of people on your trail could even be more telling than the amount of success those people have.

In the end you will not be the one determining your legacy. Your thoughts will hold little influence over how followers think about you. Instead, they will determine your legacy and they will tell stories about you to the ones who follow them. If they tell negative stories, then your legacy is one they will forget.

Establishing your legacy takes a long time

- Positive influence directly impacts legacy
- There is no benefit to a negative legacy
- People remember bad legacies much longer
- Never end professional relationships poorly
- Avoid building a legacy through social media
- Public comments can detract from your legacy

After you are gone there will be little need to talk about you either positive or negative. But what is said, how often it is shared, and the spin that is put on you, is what will determine your legacy.

6
Speaking Negatively in Public Never Works

There will be points on your leadership journey where things seem tough and you may get frustrated to the point that you cannot hold back any more. You may feel like you must say something or you will explode. Speaking out when you feel frustrated is not good form and is never necessary. Speaking out of turn during public meetings can turn out bad and negatively impact the audience and potentially the entire organization.

While preparing a large team of professionals for a critical inspection, the organization was laser focused on all aspects of physical security that would be evaluated for compliance. Success during the inspection would result in awards and promotions for many key players while failure would end careers in some cases.

The physical security team was dedicated to the success of the inspection and would dedicate every ounce of energy they could muster to make it happen. During an unfortunate period for the organization in the year before the inspection, there were major flaws discovered in areas of mandatory compliance in protection of the nation's most critical resources.

Those failed actions resulted in the firing of the previous security manager and his entire operations staff who held responsibility for the inspection preparations. The newly appointed manager had to assemble a team of experts on short-notice and get them aligned for the 73-day run before the inspection. They routinely worked 12-hour days, often staying longer, and always six days per week; taking Sunday off to spend time with family. Other teams seemed committed, but maintained a normal operations tempo.

There were many reasons to give maximum effort and work together as a team to ensure mutual support across the organization. Work schedules were adjusted to allow more hours each day to complete inspection preparations in all lines of the business. Once the organization was inside of 60 days from the inspection, regular meetings were held to get updates on progress.

The security manager and his team were responsible for many of the inspection items, but there were other teams with critical roles. Each team leader attended status meetings to provide progress across the spectrum of inspection areas. During the initial meeting there were several leaders who displayed they were not prepared, giving the impression they had not placed inspection preparations as a high priority. They provided little to no input on their efforts before the meeting.

At the next meeting, team leaders were asked to report on action items. One particular leader, whose team held a critical process was unprepared to provide updates. The boss demanded more going forward. His message was clear to everyone present; it was time to get on board and put forth maximum effort. The security manager's non-verbal reaction was not good. Some in the room waited to see if he would respond, knowing he was emotionally tied to the inspection. His frustration grew, but he withheld his thoughts, hoping everyone understood the results of a failed inspection.

At the next meeting the security manager provided updates on all tasks and gave the boss a full report on remaining items, along with the plan to complete them on time. He seemed pleased and moved on to the next team. When he got to the leader who seemed disinterested, the boss asked why a task was not complete. Instead of taking responsibility for the task, he actually turned toward the security manager and said, "His team did not tell us that it needed to be done, so this is on him."

The boss looked at the security manager, knowing how hard his team was working, and asked, "OK, why is that not done." The security manager's frustration came to fruition and he lost control of his ability to withhold comment. He said, "Sir, my team is working hard to ensure everything we own is complete, we are going 100 miles per hour to get everything done, and we don't have time to wait on people who are going 55." The entire room fell silent. The boss' facial expression indicated frustration. He slammed his notebook closed, stood up, and announced the meeting was over as he walked out. Most in the room knew that something bad just took place, while others just thought the meeting was over and they headed out. The security manager's supervisor looked at him and without speaking a word, told him they had to discuss the situation further. The manager was summoned to the boss' office for further discussion. Walking in, he was prepared to defend his position. The boss made it clear that he knew the team was working hard, and it was not his task to complete.

Then the boss got serious and told the security manager, "You are right that you don't have time to wait on people who are not fully invested in the inspection." Then he went on, "But your comment about the others going 55 miles per hour was contradictory to our success as an organization." As that sank into the manager's brain, he concluded the discussion by saying, "I am counting on you to lead your portion of the organization, but I will not tolerate you or anyone else making derogatory comments publicly." He informed the manager that he would talk to the other leader and get him on board, but that he was to never make negative comments like that in public ever again. He said, "You let your frustration get the best of you and you lost control."

The manager knew he was wrong, cleared his mind, went to visit that other leader and worked out a plan to complete all of the preparation actions that were behind schedule. Working together was the only solution to their success. The results of the inspection were historical, setting a new standard that was rarely achieved by other units. But along the way, a valuable lesson about maintaining control of one's emotions for the betterment of the team was learned.

Another Cup of My Coffee

Lesson 6

Speaking Negatively in Public Never Works

Remain in control at all times by managing what you say and when you say it

Key points for leaders:

Praise publicly and correct privately

- Saying what you think is not always smart
- Think ahead about what you are going to say
- Focus on facts in your public statements
- Eliminate raw emotion from public meetings
- Share displeasure in private rather than public
- Hold back negativity even when you are right
- Use notes to stay focused on objectives

Words matter when dealing with fellow leaders

- Speak to people with respect to maintain respect
- Control emotions during follow up discussions
- Focus on things relevant to the discussion
- You will be heard when the time is right
- Don't judge others based on what they blurt out
- Stay focused on the objectives of the conversation

Social media postings can create bad perceptions

- Being critical of others will have negative impact
- Emotional comments open people to criticism

Final Thoughts

The inability of other leaders to do their part could increase your frustration level at critical times. If other leaders are partially responsible for the success of the team, and you are depending on them to come through, patience and understanding will go a long way. Rather than speaking out publicly, you could offer to assist fellow leaders with their portion of the work to ensure the team meets its goal.

You won't get a second chance to make a good impression. If you make a bad impression in a public meeting, people will remember it for a long time.

Always maintain your poise in public settings

- Your character will be viewed by how you act
- People will respect you and your inputs
- Remain as positive as possible in public forums

You don't always know or understand the other leader's challenges. Take some time to get with them and discuss what may be going on. This mutual effort could lead to a solution. Keep yourself in check at all times and don't speak out negatively.

7
Deliver on Your Promises

A leader is in charge and has responsibility. There is normally formal recognition of this fact, it's stated publicly, and people understand the hierarchy of the organization. Everyone knows who is in charge. But a leader must also establish credibility in their position so that people respect what they do and how they do it. If you establish credibility, people will respect your decisions, even in the toughest of times.

During a difficult period of the war in Iraq, the command chief was responsible for ensuring standards were maintained and that people who deployed to the combat zone were well trained for the job they would perform. They needed to be physically and mentally prepared for the duties under difficult conditions. Each person was scrutinized by leadership, evaluated by medical teams, and had to demonstrate their physical fitness by completing a formal test, meeting a minimum passing score before they could deploy.

The individual fitness score was one of the only criteria that was considered black and white. If you passed, you were allowed to deploy. If you failed, it normally meant that someone else would take your place. The fact is, someone who is not physically fit enough to complete and pass the basic fitness test under normal conditions, would present a high likelihood of failure under the stress and conditions of combat and be a liability to the unit.

During the troop surge of 2007, additional forces rapidly deployed, requiring additional leaders to guide them. It became difficult to fill all of those positions with highly qualified and motivated individuals because of the time crunch. Enlisted leadership positions were critical to the success of the mission as they were front and center with the troops on the ground. Leaders would have to work long days, handle stress, and lead with courage under difficult conditions.

The command chief in Iraq received a call from a peer who was stationed back in the U.S. They knew each other from previous missions and had formed a trusting relationship over the years. Brian was straight forward and honest in the conversation. He began by sharing that he had a leader who would be deploying to Iraq under the surge. He stated that he was the right person for the job, that he had all the necessary job qualifications, was a strong leader, and had proven himself under difficult conditions. "There was only one problem," Brian said. He shared that because the leader failed to pass his fitness test by a few points he was disqualified from the deployment. The phone went silent as the command chief pondered where the conversation was going next. He simply said, "Okay, so why are we talking now." Brian went on to say, "I believe in this leader, and I believe that he can and will do the job he is tasked for."

The command chief asked Brian to share more about the leader so that he could fully understand the situation.

Brian detailed the qualifications of the leader and what he thought he could do to positively impact the mission and motivate the troops. Happy to hear those things, the command chief told Brian that there was still this requirement to have passed the fitness test so that we could be assured that he would not fail under the stress of combat and become a liability to the unit. Brian said, "Chief, I am so confident in his ability to perform and not fail, that I will make you this promise; if he fails, you can call me up and I will have my combat gear packed and ready to go. Without question, I will get on the next plane, deploy to Iraq, and take his place."

That was not what the command chief was expecting, but it sounded intriguing. This trusted fellow leader was telling him that he was willing to give up his current duties, leave his family, and put himself in harm's way if the person he was recommending for deployment failed to perform under extreme conditions. The command chief thought it sounded like a low risk proposition.

The command chief told Brian that he would accept his offer and waive the fitness requirement because of his personal commitment and established credibility. The command chief ended the call by telling Brian to keep his bag packed, because he would not hesitate to uphold the agreement. Brian thanked the command chief for believing in him and promised that while his bag would be packed, there would be no need to use it because the leader he was sending to war would not fail.

Over the next six months the unit leader who deployed to combat became one of the strongest on the base. He was fully engaged in daily combat operations, provided direct support for senior leaders, and motivated troops on the front lines. He worked tirelessly to complete difficult tasks under direct enemy fire. His performance and commitment were never in question.

Months later the command chief saw Brian during a brief respite from Iraq at a leadership conference. Brian's first question for the command chief was about the performance of the unit leader he sent forward. The chief told him that it was going extremely well and that his promise was being upheld. He told Brian that his trust and confidence never wavered and the leadership skills he demonstrated were crucial to the completion of the mission.

The command chief thanked Brian for putting his credibility on the line and guaranteeing results. It was only because of the previously established credibility that the door was opened. That credibility meant everything in the decision process. If this same call came from someone who did not have the level of credibility that Brian had, this story would never have happened.

Another Cup of My Coffee

Lesson 7

Deliver on Your Promises

Your leadership credibility will grow when you follow through on your commitments

Key points for leaders:

Earn credibility through your personal actions

- Trust people who have earned credibility
- Proven performance grows credibility
- Earn credibility by upholding your promises
- Sustain proven performance over long periods
- Performance under stress builds credibility

Others determine your credibility rating

- Credibility must exist at all leadership levels
- Don't put your credibility on the line lightly
- Surround yourself with credible people
- Expect scrutiny of your decisions
- Accept consequences of your promises
- Trust is essential to back up your actions

Final Thoughts

If a leader fails to prove themselves over time by not following through on their promises, people will lose confidence in them and stop following. This lack of followership will lead to negative organizational norms, destructive behavior, and focus on individual survival. Leaders who lack credibility will struggle to gain the confidence of their superiors. The organization will lose when this situation is present.

Leaders must correct loss of confidence

- Own failures and be willing to discuss them
- Deflecting the failure to others will not work
- Ignoring the failure will not make it go away
- Recover from failure by taking positive action

Finally, when a leader takes the word of another who has placed their credibility on the line, that leader is also taking a risk. If the situation goes bad, and there is a loss of credibility, the leader's own credibility will take a hit. If the leader in this story had failed, the command chief's credibility could have been called into question. Others would have criticized him for waiving the fitness requirement.

8
Influence One Person at a Time

As a leader you will be many things to your organization and the people you are responsible for leading. Over the course of your career there will be many celebratory moments in leadership. But there will also be many periods of struggle, frustration, and a desire to quit. Some leaders find it difficult to influence people toward organizational goals more than on their own individual goals. It may be difficult to convince people that working toward mission accomplishment will pay more dividends than working toward their personal goals. The leader must clarify the vision of the organization, motivate individuals to work for the team, and effectively communicate. While it may be difficult to ingrain a team-first mentality, leaders must drive individual performance to achieve great things.

During combat deployments, military members get satisfaction and fulfillment from the mission they have been tasked to accomplish. Long and difficult days are followed by detailed de-briefings, equipment and vehicle maintenance, nourishment, sleep, and hygiene. Those activities leave little time for much else. But those same people are so motivated and used to the long days that when they have a few hours of free time, they look for other meaningful things to accomplish. Idle time leads to depression from missing loved ones and unacceptable behaviors that lead to corrective or disciplinary actions. They like to be busy and productive and leaders benefit from the focus on meaningful opportunities.

During the worst statistical months of the war in Iraq, leaders often found people looking for ways to fill a few hours each week with productive activities. Senior leaders had to remain engaged with their people both on and off duty to ensure they maintained focus. Because of that need, professional development courses were conducted when the mission did not demand the full attention from font-line troops. These courses were conducted at no cost to the attendees and delivered by experienced leaders who hoped to grow the leadership skills of their followers.

One of the most active groups consisted of mid-level supervisors who were already in leadership positions, having responsibility for front line people. In addition to completing their own duties they were also accountable for team performance, safety, and reliability. They spent so much of their time coaching, mentoring, and directing others, it left little time for themselves, including their own development.

A command chief whose responsibility spanned the entire countryside returned from a long day of travel to forward operating bases where he spent time with front line combat forces. Once back at the base, the command chief and the commanding general stopped by to see a gathering of warriors who just completed a professional development course. There was food and drink to help celebrate course completion. As the event was winding down, the formal leader of this group cornered the command chief and expressed her concerns for recent decreases in participation at professional development courses. She was frustrated that her efforts to organize and conduct events seemed to be going to waste and that she was not having influence on people the way she intended. As she continued, her emotions took over and she grew even more frustrated with the situation. At one point she told the command chief, "I just don't feel like I am making a difference for anyone and it makes me want to quit."

The command chief listened intently while she carried on. She said, "How am I supposed to influence and impact these people if they don't show up." The command chief moved closer to her, ensuring her full attention was on what he was about to say. Then he lifted the index finger on his right hand and said, "One person at a time." She stopped breathing momentarily. Time stood still as she looked at him, waiting to hear more. Then she asked, "What do you mean, one person at a time?" The command chief told her, "You influence one person at a time. Stop trying to influence the entire group, as they may not be motivated in the same way you are. Stop being frustrated by those who do not want to be influenced positively. Focus all of your effort on that one person who shows a desire to learn and grow."

The command chief turned and walked away, looking back to ensure she was OK. The look on her faced showed understanding, and seemed to kick her back into high gear and she started directing others to wrap things up and get back to work. That simple statement of "one person at a time" made immediate sense to her. It was the reminder that any and all effort to positively influence others is worthwhile. If a leader makes a genuine effort to influence others and only one or two people catch on, the time and energy are well spent. The reassurance she gained from the simple guidance ignited her to lead and influence without getting frustrated. During her remaining time in the combat zone she performed every aspect of her duties with conviction. She was highly engaged with those around her and it was obvious.

Her direct influence made a huge impact on many lives, one person at a time. By the end of her combat tour, although exhausted from pouring out so much energy to help others, she went home fulfilled. She was a highly respected leader, mentor, and influencer who positively impacted many others, one person at a time.

Another Cup of My Coffee

Lesson 8

Influence One Person at a Time

Don't spend time trying to influence people who have no desire to learn and grow

<u>Key points for leaders:</u>

Power or position don't influence people

- Respected leaders influence the most people
- Let your actions influence others indirectly
- Actions are evaluated more than words
- Leaders are always being emulated
- Leadership is not a part-time job
- Lead with excellence and people will follow

Not everyone wants you to influence them

- Influence is not automatic or guaranteed
- People determine if they accept your influence
- You cannot force influence if it is not desired
- Forceful influence will turn people away
- Public influence on social media has no value

Final Thoughts

A leader who attempts to influence others based solely on positional authority will find that impact is lessoned…it will be weak at best. Rather, a leader should use their natural ability to influence and motivate people toward goals by growing their relationship. When you find someone who shows a desire to be influenced and learn, give them additional time and attention.

Once you try to force influence on people who are unwilling, you will likely never get the chance to reverse their feelings toward you. Resentment will run high, and your leadership impact will be diminished.

Never say, "I am about to influence you."

- Natural charisma will draw people toward you
- Speaking only when necessary creates respect
- Credibility in your words will impact positively
- Be clear and concise in your communications
- Respect is not earned through self-admiration

Leaders of high moral character will be followed and admired by people who they have little or no direct influence over. Your character alone can influence people who observe you without personal interaction. They learn from you and emulate that behavior, without ever having a conversation with you. Leaders are always on the clock. Everything you say is heard, everything you do is seen.

9
Be Slow to Judge

Leaders like to be in tune with their people and their surroundings and know what is going on at all times. Understanding the people who make up the organization creates a better sense of awareness and can drive positive interactions. However, sometimes the circumstances presented at the moment appear different than they really are, and to ensure success, you have to be slow to determine the intentions of a person until you know and understand all the details.

While serving in a combat environment under the constant threat of attack, there was little time for fun and less time for joking around. Each person who arrived in country was expected to hit the ground running, learn their job, understand the rules of engagement, and get to work with a high level of situational awareness. Bases often came under attack as relief forces arrived.

It was important for leaders to maintain the highest level of awareness and enforce the same standard for everyone involved in the mission. Often that meant early encounters with troops within hours of arrival. The command chief led the effort to meet troops where they arrived in large groups to set the tone while they picked up their gear. It was a large gathering area that had little protection from incoming fire. The operation could drag on for hours, but every effort was made to move it along quickly and get people away from the easily targeted area.

The chief was passing by the gathering area and noticed three new troops who seemed to be milling about aimlessly so he approached to see if he could help. The team leader made it clear they were looking for a lost bag but did not need assistance. As the chief and team leader discussed the situation, the other two warriors continued looking for the bag among hundreds that were strewn about. The chief was excited to see them since they were security force members, his former career field. He held them in high esteem and understood the difficulty of their mission to defend the base under daily enemy attacks. It was a critical career field that required the highest level of professionalism and awareness.

After the short conversation the chief looked toward the others and asked if they had any luck finding their bags so they could move on and get ready for their jobs. One of them turned around and began laughing loudly. Confused by his reaction, the chief asked the young man if he found something funny in what he said. The young warrior responded by saying, "No, sir." And again, he started to laugh out loud. The chief became instantly infuriated, as he did not like being laughed at when he was trying to help them. He wondered how someone from security forces could be so cavalier about the situation and laugh at a senior leader. The chief approached to find out more about why he was laughing.

As the chief drew closer the young man began laughing even louder. Again the chief asked if he found something funny in what he said. On hearing the question the young man laughed even louder, seeming unable to control his actions. The chief got up close to the young man and asked directly, "Do you think I am funny?" After a short pause and more laughing, the chief said, "Are you laughing at something I said?" The young man was able to compose himself for a moment so he could reply, "No sir, nothing is funny." This chief asked, "Then why are you laughing every time I speak to you?" The situation came to a head when the young man said, "I'm not laughing at you chief." At that moment his team leader stepped in to speak with the chief and hopefully calm him down.

Stepping away so they could have a private discussion, the team leader told him, "Chief, he cannot control his laughter, he has a laughing disorder." Standing speechless for a second, the chief told him that there was no such thing as a laughing disorder and that he was just trying to cover for his team member. The team leader tried once again to inform the chief that his team member was inflicted with a laughing disorder, and that when he gets nervous, he laughs even louder. Still not convinced, the chief decided to slow down and ask the next question. He wanted to understand something he had never heard of and get a full explanation. The chief said, "You mean the madder I get with him the more he will laugh at me?" The team leader said, "Exactly."

The chief was a combat-tested leader who thought he was totally aware of everything around him and could handle any situation he encountered, but this was different. He found it hard to believe that a person could actually have an infliction that would be portrayed as laughter when he felt stressed. The chief also didn't want to believe that his actions and words caused the problem to get worse. The chief needed to gather his thoughts because he was in unfamiliar territory.

Once he was satisfied that this situation was real, he turned to the young man and wished him well during his combat tour. The humbled chief told him that if he was unable to find his bag, he should come by and see him later in the day. They parted ways and the chief shook his head in near disbelief, as he just realized that he did not know everything there was to know about people. He also understood that by being so quick to judge the young man he failed to understand his total surroundings and remain in total awareness.

From that day forward, the chief tried hard not to determine circumstances of a situation until he had full awareness of the facts. His own situational awareness was raised to a new level because of the young man who laughed at him for no apparent reason. Throughout the months that followed, he encountered that young man many times, and each time he became more comfortable, nearly eliminating the laughter all together.

Another Cup of My Coffee

Lesson 9

Be Slow to Judge

Find out everything you can before criticizing people's actions

<u>Key points for leaders:</u>

Withhold comment on unusual situations

- Gain full awareness of circumstances around you
- Don't comment unless absolutely required
- Use non-judgmental comments or questions
- Ask thought-provoking questions
- Listen carefully, reflect on words, respond properly

Realize you don't know everything

- Figure out what you don't know
- Seek information from others who have insight
- What else can you know about a person's life
- Support the situation with positive behavior
- Offer to assist with fixing issues within your control
- Show compassion for people and their circumstances

Final Thoughts

Getting to know your people will take a huge investment of time and energy. But the results of knowing and understanding them will pay great dividends. Successful leaders gain perspective on people of all walks, all abilities, and all inflictions. They remain open to the benefits of a diversified workforce and learn to appreciate everyone for their contribution.

Leaders who jump into conversations and make determinations without understanding the full scope of the situation are subject to failure. Your ability to lead people and impact teams will be negatively impacted by your lack of awareness and perceived irrational or erratic behavior.

Jumping into a conversation creates problems

- People may be unintentionally offended
- Communication roadblocks will be erected
- Social media postings can damage relationships
- Adversarial relationships can be formed
- Trust and confidence are broken down

Most people situations are not time critical, allowing you to gather sufficient information to make a good determination of what is going on. If you rush to judgement, you will say something wrong or offensive.

10
Deliberate Actions Create Efficiency

Time and effort are valuable pieces of every leader's life. You only have so much time to live, to work, and to be with the ones you love. Effort is easy when you are young, but gets tougher as life gets more complicated and your responsibility grows. Knowing how to make the most out of your time and effort is a valuable lesson every leader can benefit from. Using your time effectively and making smart use of your effort will pay great dividends. As a leader you will dedicate time to contribute to organizational goals, fulfilling your own responsibilities, and taking care of your followers. Time management will be an important piece of your leadership approach.

Opportunities to learn are available every day from those we follow, people in our lives, and others coaches and mentors. Leaders can be found at work, on teams, and often at home while a person is growing up. Sometimes, a father or mother can teach a valuable lesson that will impact a leader later in their life. Leadership lessons are often taught through deliberate actions viewed from experienced people who care about their followers.

A young boy destined to become a senior military leader learned a valuable lesson about efficiency from his father, one of the earliest and best teachers of his life. His father was a master mechanic and talented machinist who could always be found in his shop working on another project. Although the young boy had a busy schedule with school and sports, he spent many nights in the shop watching and learning from his dad as he built vehicles and completed a variety of other mechanical projects. The boy's help was normally limited to gathering tools, moving things, or cleaning up the shop.

He understood the value of cleaning the shop as his dad and brother worked, allowing them to stay focused on the task at hand. The boy's ability to get tools from the tool box and return quickly with them allowed the others to remain under the vehicle, or wherever they were working at the moment. Even before the world learned to "lean" down their processes, the boy seemed to understand the value of saving time and effort in that shop while helping his dad.

The boy knew that if he dedicated himself to knowing tools by their name, it would save time in retrieving them when needed. He understood that his efficiency would save time and frustration when working on a critical portion of an engine rebuild or some other crucial job. He knew that when his dad asked for a tool he wanted it quick, so he needed to be locked in.

On one particular night his dad and brother were under a time crunch to get a go-kart ready for an early morning departure to compete in a huge race. Things were not going as planned, and stress levels ran high. Grabbing a tool and responding back to the area, the boy stood at the ready. When his dad was done with a tool and handed it to him, he laid it on the ground, wanting to be ready to get whatever came next. Moments later his dad moved in his direction to get a better angle and stepped on the tool previously laid on the ground. His dad asked why it was there and not back in the tool box. As the boy moved the tool out of the way, he told his dad that he was trying to save time by not leaving his side, and that he would pick it up later. His dad said, "You just moved it a second time and later will need to move it a third time." Not wanting to add to the stress of the night, the boy just brushed over the comment and focused on the moment.

Soon after his dad asked him to start cleaning up so they could test the engine. The boy moved things from the immediate area and pushed them away from the engine stand. His dad's look changed to frustration about what the boy was doing, but he was working so hard that he didn't have time to address him. The engine started on the first try and it seemed they would be ready in time to leave for the race. It was now time to clean up the entire shop and get things loaded for the trip.

The boy began cleaning the shop and putting things back in their place. What should have taken mere minutes, drug into a half hour. His dad came back into the shop to find him still cleaning things up and asked why it was taking so long. The boy told him it was a hard job and there were things laying all over the shop. At that moment his dad said, "If you move something once, it may take longer at the moment, but will save you time later." He went on to explain that if the boy had put the tools away each time he was done with one, they would not have been laying around the shop, cutting down his time to clean up and making the area safe to work in.

The boy thought for a minute and knew his dad was right. If you don't move something back to its intended place the first time, you will have to move it again. Therefore, why not move it once! Seemed simple, and would relate to saving time and effort. He knew from that day forward that he would become a completer, and always see things through with deliberate actions. That lesson would last a lifetime and play a huge role in how he would guide his professional life.

Another Cup of My Coffee

Lesson 10

Deliberate Actions Create Efficiency

Moving things once will save time in the long run

<u>Key points for leaders:</u>

Efficient actions save time and money

- Include efficiency in the organizational culture
- Plan things out before starting your operations
- Stay organized by keeping things in their place
- Establish good practices to improve processes
- Remain open to ideas for process improvement
- Efficient use of people adds to organizational morale

Lack of efficiency wastes time and money

- Duplication of effort causes frustration
- Valuable production time is wasted
- Shortcuts are used to make up for lost time
- Safety procedures may be compromised

Final Thoughts

Successful industries have determined there is great value in streamlining operations. Studies have found that if you save seconds during an operation that is repeated thousands of times each week, you save thousands of seconds. This time savings relates to increased productivity, reduced man-hours, and increased revenue.

Make good use of the free time you create

- Walk around the organization with no purpose
- Meet with people and discuss their successes
- Talk with peers to collaborate on new ideas
- Spend some time reading professional material

Leaders have many demands on their time and saving a few minutes each week may not seem like much. However, over time those seconds will add up to productivity in other areas of your day.

Lesson 1:
Slow Down and Ask the Next Question

Take the time to gather appropriate information before
taking dangerous or serious actions

Lesson 2:
Relevance Begins with Presence

Leaders must be seen and heard to have impact

Lesson 3:
You Have Been So Advised

Advise your leaders with positive intent to impact their
decisions

Lesson 4:
Courage is a Great Motivator

Do not worry about other people judging you

Lesson 5:
Other People Determine Your Legacy

Opinions are formed based on how they see you perform

Lesson 6:
Speaking Negatively in Public Never Works

Remain in control at all times by managing what you say
and when you say it

Lesson 7:
Deliver on Your Promises

Your leadership credibility will grow when you follow
through on your commitments

Lesson 8:
Influence One Person at a Time

Don't spend time trying to influence people who have no
desire to learn and grow

Lesson 9:
Be Slow to Judge

Find out everything you can before criticizing people's
actions

Lesson 10:
Deliberate Actions Create Efficiency

Moving things once will save time in the long run

ABOUT THE AUTHOR

Scott H. Dearduff retired from the United States Air Force in January 2011 as Command Chief Master Sergeant for Ninth Air Force and United States Air Forces Central Command. He deployed more than 1000 days to combat operations in the Central Command Area of Operations, including Iraq and Afghanistan. He served in more than 20 countries around the world and has traveled to more than 50 foreign countries. His leadership skills were honed under fire  during nuclear security operations, Presidential security, disaster relief operations, humanitarian relief, aircraft accidents and an active shooter response with mass casualties. He holds a Bachelor's Degree in Management. His military decorations include the Legion of Merit, 3 Bronze Star Medals, Afghanistan and Iraq Campaign Medals with multiple service stars, and the Air Force Combat Action Medal among more than 27 total decorations. He is the recipient of the James M. Shamess Award for Literary Excellence, the Bronze Patrick Henry Medallion for Patriotism, the Patriot Award from the Employer Support of the Guard and Reserve, and was named a Distinguished Alumni from Spruce Creek High School in Florida. His memoires from Iraq, *Chief*, is listed on the 2017 Air Force Chief of Staff's professional reading list.

Contact the Chief at dearduffconsulting@gmail.com

Other books available on Amazon:
Chief, My Journey Thru Iraq at the Peak of War
A Cup of My Coffee, Lessons for Life
A Cup of My Coffee 2, Military Lessons for Business Leaders
A Cup of My Coffee 3, Lessons for Military Leaders
A Cup of My Coffee 4, Lessons for Everyday Life
A Cup of My Coffee 5-0, Lessons for Law Enforcement Leaders